Table of Contents

INTRODUCTION

If you recently ended a relationship, you undoubtedly want to know how to make your ex miss you. There are many reasons why relationships end. A normal argument might result in an unexpected split. It seems sense that you would miss and desire to visit your ex if you had a long-term relationship. But because you are unsure about your ex's mental health, you could be reluctant to initiate contact.

There are a few things you can do to make your ex miss you more so that they will want to get in touch with you. Breakups are very difficult, and it's common for couples to have withdrawal symptoms after a split.

Always unpleasant and violent, breakups are. You had a really difficult time with your ex. The moment has come to repay that courtesy. The suffering they forced you to endure is inexcusable and immeasurable. Therefore, it is crucial that you help them understand how painful heartbreak is. We'll talk about several strategies in this book for making your ex envious and making them beg for your pardon. So read this book if you want to find out how to make your ex jealous.

When you are going through a split and still wanting to get back together with your ex, it is reasonable to think about ways to make them miss you. During a breakup, you may experience contradictory emotions and wish for your ex's company, calls, or messages while also hoping that they would miss you. These are a few strategies for making them miss you and, if there is a possibility, for reconciling. If there is no longer any interest, it is always preferable to move on and develop into a better version of yourself. Continue reading to learn some advice on how to make your ex miss you and want to reconcile.

The most crucial thing is that you have to execute it correctly to avoid coming across as desperate. And you must strictly adhere to the advice in this book if you don't want the ball to end up in your court.

But how exactly can you make your ex envious? There are various approaches, but there are only a select number that are effective. I will now provide some of the most beneficial and practical techniques for reaching your goals.

This is an intriguing subject that has given rise to a very modern phenomenon when couples argue online or in real life. One of the most well-known varieties is using social media to avenge partners who have likely dumped them.

However, women typically excel at this game, particularly on platforms like Facebook, Whatsapp, Instagram, and any others that are at their disposal. But who's to say that men can't likewise exact revenge on their ex-partners who treated them badly?

Well, in my opinion, there are a variety of ways to avenge an ex, including making them crave you repeatedly and even want to be in your arms once more.

If you genuinely want to make that spouse envious, you're obviously an SNG. One thing I can guarantee is that if you play your cards right and use the tricks and techniques discussed in this article well, then be reassured of results that would blow your mind. After all, the fact that you're here reading this book shows me that you're already well aware that using jealousy is a good way to make your ex feel attracted to you again and make her want you back.

No matter how harsh they may be, nobody really wants to watch their ex-partners out on dates and having a good time nearly almost away after the breakup. Instead of seeing a dejected spouse at home pleading with them, show them that you're out having fun with dates, and sooner or later they'll text or phone you.

Show them that you still wish them well and desire the best for them despite the fact that you two are no longer together. The idea here is reverse psychology; when you phone and email them well wishes, post photographs of incredibly attractive females on social media wishing them well as well as how much fun it is to get out with them. They'll be drawn to you once again as a result of this, for sure.

The Most Frequent Causes Of Breakups Are:

- Emergence Of Bothersome Or Negative Behaviors
- Putting On Or Shedding Pounds
- Dating Other People
- Become Unappreciative Or Neglectful
- Lies And Dishonesty

1.

HANG OUT WITH YOUR FUCKING FRIENDS/OPPOSITE SEX

Develop a habit of hanging out with your pals or opposite sex dress up well, take some fun photos, and take her to a restaurant or somewhere she's always wanted to go with you, alone, or with her friends. This also draws her attention. Remember, your purpose is to make her envious.

Making new pals of the opposite gender might make your ex envious. Remember when you weren't allowed to get out with your friends because you were in a relationship?

You are now free and have no one to answer to. Take advantage of the chance to make your ex feel uneasy. They used to know your connecting with your pals really well, but in the case of a new buddy, they don't, and they know nothing about them. Make new acquaintances and expand your social activities or cycle, but don't break links with old ones unless they are harmful.

It is more difficult for an elderly person to allow someone into their personal space. You can begin with your coworkers. For example, try shortening the gap with a few lovely folks from your company and suggesting getting out for coffee after a long day at work. Take a few photographs and share them on social media if appropriate.

However, be certain that your buddy does not feel any pressure from you. When making new acquaintances, you should be genuine and not only to show your ex how well you spend your time away from them.

New pals will provide new experiences and assist shift the attention away from previous relationships and onto exciting times in the present.

This will pique your ex's interest and make him nervous. They will also gain an understanding of how far you have progressed in your life. They no longer have a place in your life.

Share photos of her perceived rivalry while you were together.

Share images of yourself with the lady and publish them on social media; she saw it as a competition when you were together.

Ex-girlfriends will be envious if you show how happy and calm you are in the company of other women. If you're always conversing with other females, she'll feel ignored and wonder if you still care about her.

You are not required to date other ladies or have sexual relations here. You're just having fun with the other gals. Socializing in this manner is beneficial to both you and your ex.

Meeting new people and establishing new friends can boost your confidence and allow you to improve. This will also demonstrate your ability to form your own social network.

What's more! It might keep you away from folks you wish to avoid so they don't get to always bring her topic up or how good the two of you were, as at the time of dating, which most times weaken your resolve to achieve your ultimate plans.

The fact that many people become extremely furious anytime they see their ex-partner with someone else is an unfortunately well-known reality. If someone perceives an emotional link between their ex and his or her new boyfriend, they become even more envious. Anyway, you've come to the perfect spot if you want to rekindle your ex-jealousy partner's but don't know how to go about it.

Try to find a method to appear cheerful and look beautiful. Spend time with your friends, have fun, treat yourself to something new, or get that item you've been eyeing. And even if none of these strategies succeed, always go around with a grin on your face. After a breakup, it's acceptable to feel sad for a few weeks or even months, but never let your ex know how you're feeling. Don't let them run your life and dictate your attitude.

Spending time with your common friends is a unique way to attract your ex's attention. They are both familiar with each other and can play a significant role in communicating your current viewpoints and ideas to your ex-partner. Your ex-partner will probably question them about you even if they don't. So go ahead and spend as much time as you can with them. You have a good possibility of learning the tricks of how to make your ex jealous and perhaps win him or her back, so go ahead and spill the beans to your common pals about every juicy little detail.

Note: taking out time with friends is important in a breakup process because it take away the moment of what I call "self-alone" it may sound unreal but that period is really a difficult stage because its always the first stage, where all you get to witness all around you is the love others share and how perfect they seem. In this stage is where you need your close friends more to hold you on and guard you or even encourage you to move on. But this book isn't to just move on but to get your partner jealous and bring them into your life.

So to really achieve these in this book, we need no dull moment we you to be active and responsive to accomplish our goal.

Also your friends doesn't have to be of the same sex, it good you try creating a different vibes around yourself, where they will see the pain or torture you are going through, I never said you should get involve with someone at any given opportunity, because you will look like too desperate and hurt yourself the more.

Going out with the opposite sex to his/her favorite spot or bar will make your ex see how much good and happy you are and how much she is missing, especially when she noticed your date smiling and looking good, talking to your eyes and laughing, you have just unlock their burning desires, all this actions of your is to get them to be jealous.

I know of a friend did this to his ex-girlfriend who broke-up with him and when she noticed him with a different date sitting at their favorite spot in bar, despite she came to the bar with a male friend or her date she couldn't sit, eat or drink, all she could see was the way he was talking to his date in her ears, biting his lips, holding her hand and playing with it, how he was holding his drink, and how joyful they both look, she was forced to leave her date and walk up to her ex and ask for them to talk. Now they are both back and she doesn't joke with him anymore.

Your case may be different from my friend but if you are determine to get your spouse back putting these technique into practice you will get them.

But this isn't a sure way because human's actions and behavior differ so your result may differ too in certain way.

2.

BECOME A BETTER VERSION OF YOU

When a female dumps a guy, it typically happens because she found another guy she thinks is twice as good as you or because the guy isn't performing well enough. However, the majority of the time, guys strive to outdo the new guy or entirely change their ways to become the "Mumu" that the female desires. This is a false impression; instead of attempting to out the new man or switching to a "Mumu," work on increasing your sense of confidence and self-worth. Get out there, reinvent yourself, and follow your aspirations and goals while watching women scurry to your feet as you become a better version of yourself.

It makes sense that you would have gotten to know one other's families and shared a social circle if you had been dating for a while and were in a committed relationship. You both participate in every event, from family picnics and Thanksgiving feasts to your closest friend's baby shower.

After a breakup, it might be challenging to keep your distance from friends and family. Their presence in your life may serve as a continual reminder of the split and the separation of the parties. You will undoubtedly think of your ex whenever you interact with any of them in person or receive a call from them.

Minor triggers might cause recollections of the relationship to flood your mind after the split. You have adored everything about them and known them through and out. The melody of their favorite music, a smell of the perfume they used to wear, the sight of their favorite café every time you pass past it. All these triggers will transport you back to the happy times you had and the lovely memories you made after the split. They remain ingrained in your memory.

They've filled your gallery to the brim with pictures. They serve as regular reminders of what has been lost and is missing from your life, from your private photos to your humorous forwards. These pictures serve as a reminder of a happier moment in your lives.

Everyone, including you, has terrible habits. Is there anything about you that your ex-partner disliked? It might be something little, such as chewing one's nails or being unorganized or untidy, or it can be something major, such as bad voice modulation or dressed like a homeless woman. Whatever it may be, you need to change or eliminate your undesirable behaviors. Improve your personality and work on yourself. Maintain your comfort and cleanliness at all times. Get in shape, look nice, and lose belly fat. Girl, do whatever it takes! When your ex-partner first sees you, they'll notice right away that you've changed, which will undoubtedly make them envious!

You will gain fresh perspectives on yourself and your personality as a result of this technique. When your ex sees that you are having fun taking up a pastime and enjoying yourself, they will miss you.

Sexual activity and physical intimacy are a given in committed relationships. In the immediate aftermath of a breakup, you could miss your partner's touch, warmth, and physical tenderness in addition to just seeing them. A sudden absence of it might be challenging to handle and make lovers badly miss one other.

Yes, the sensation is awful. And now that you are aware that your ex may be missing you just as much, there are a number of things you may do to get them back. However, it's not as easy as it seems.

You cannot force your ex to miss you and desire to rekindle your relationship. You must allow them time to completely understand their sentiments and emotions since it is a long process. Your absence will trouble them once they start to sense their actual affections for you.

Find a new activity that your ex is unaware of. By doing so, you'll demonstrate to him that you're more than he realizes. You should frequently record your hobby-related activities and broadcast them to the world. It's impossible to overstate how much of an impact it will have on your ex.

Take care of yourself and keep yourself in mind. Make good eating and lifestyle decisions rather than giving in to your feelings and overindulging in junk food or comfort food. Your ex will be drawn to you if you feel good about yourself since it will show in your demeanor.

You may make some improvements to get your loved one back, whether they relate to looks or conduct (e.g., smoking). For instance, it's common practice for guys to pamper themselves and work out in order to enhance their appearance and make women regret leaving them. Women may also improve their looks with haircuts, new clothes, and even tattoos.

Making a positive adjustment can not only increase your chances of getting your ex back but also raise your self-worth and perhaps even your health.

Becoming a better version of yourself is very essential to regaining your power back, let your old self go and become a new person in the way you walk, talk, eat, play, friends you keep, basically your action and thinking.

- **You Need To Change the Way and Manner You Dress**: you dressing tells a lot about you, either you are still your old self or a reformed man or woman. Why do I need to change the way I dress because it's the first thing anyone notice about you before coming close to you. It's tells a significant amount of story about your personality from a far distance. Perception is everything.
  Wear quality well-made clothing. They send an instant message that you know what you're doing.
- **Smell Good And Sexy**: when one come close to you after looking good you are to follow their inner most desire by smell good that everyone will want to know who has just passed me and even after you are way good you fragrance still stay, throw away all those cheap ass perfume, the don't do u any good. Even if you are trying to get or attract someone for the first time, it show how classic you are. Same thing could be applied in business, it makes you look expensive and serious. Your reputation should precede you. And its tells your partners this individual has really change, they will be wondering what really happened while am away.
- **Change Your Hair Style**: your hair style should also tell a story about you, that you are ready to exploit every aspect of life. You hair cut/style is what tell other is you responsible or not.
- **Eat And Wine In An Expensive Bar**: this technique shouldn't be used always but just do it regardless of the pain make your spouse feel they are missing something get.
- **Read Good Books .**
- **Learn To Encourage Others.**

3.

HAVING A POSITIVE EMOTION

Say some kind things to your ex and give them compliments to make them feel good. You might even make out. Then, after raising some interest in more, go into hiding and stop communicating for a while.

You can take a lesson from someone leaving you when they did so. Keep in mind how self-petty they made you feel. the way they use absurd justifications to end things with you.

You now have the chance to truly tell them what they have lost. You must recognize your value in order to do it. You must demonstrate to them that you are a driven and career-oriented individual.

You may strive every day and every night toward the goals you have for the future. They are unfortunate not to be a part of your trip, and Nobody can prevent you from pursuing your aspirations, either.

Create a feeling of anticipation and want for her, and then stop communicating your thoughts or actions to her.

Use one of the other suggestions on this page after a week or two, so she keeps getting conflicting signals while complimenting her buddy.

Many grieving lovers do a frequent error by continuing to communicate with an ex-girlfriend or ex-boyfriend after a split. But why would anyone keep in touch with someone who has already abandoned them? Basically, there are two possibilities: either they split up amicably or they still harbor feelings for their ex. Couples that have been together for a long time are probably more likely to experience the second situation.

What's the big deal about this? They know you're still responsible if you stay in touch with a love partner who dumped you. And when something is simple to obtain, it almost completely loses its appeal.

Your ex is undoubtedly certain that you will be inconsolable when they go. Don't give them that much joy. Although you are sad and embarrassed, your ex doesn't need to be aware of it.

Aim to grin more frequently. Be kind and pleasant. You will first need to persuade yourself or even act as though everything is alright until it ultimately becomes true.

You want your ex to think that you are moving on happily and aren't hurting from the split. How do you go about doing that? Many people look desperately for a new date in order to make their ex-partner envious. It's not always the best course of action, though.

Generally speaking, flirting is a harmless action that individuals engage in, but how can you make your ex jealous if they start flirting with others? You shouldn't be envious in this situation since it would be the worst error you could ever make. Don't even consider being impolite or obscene. If you do happen to run into the couple by chance, just shake their hands. Make a clever remark to the new lady or even bring up how they make a cute couple.

Start establishing a more cordial connection. After a brief introduction and brief dialogue, continue the conversation with him/her for 10 to 20minutes. However, make sure you always say goodbye before letting him/her stay any longer than he/she wishes to. They will be much more upset to see you depart as a result. After that, wait for them to invite you to get a coffee or, if you're feeling courageous, ask them for a drink.

Given no indication to him/her that you wish to date him again. Just seem very charming and fantastic, and they'll want to hang out with you again.

You must learn to have a positive mindset, change the way and manner you think. Understand how your partner feels of is feeling. Note that your partner has feeling and emotion and the world doesn't revolve around only on you.

Positive emotions alter our brains in ways that broaden our awareness, attention, and memory instead of restricting it, as do negative emotions. They let us to process more information and keep numerous concepts in mind simultaneously.

Make positive feelings outweigh negative ones.

It is simpler to face challenging circumstances when we experience more happy emotions than negative ones. Our resilience is increased by joyful feelings (the emotional resources needed for coping). They increase our awareness and let us notice additional choices for fixing problems.

Every day, cultivate positivity.

We may become happier, perform better, and experience a reduction in our negative emotions by developing behaviors that promote us to feel more good emotions. If we are already coping with a lot of negative emotions like heart break, fear, sorrow, anger, irritation, or stress, it is extremely crucial to develop good emotions.

Positive feelings are healthy for you and make you feel happy. Pay attention to these effective tools and figure out how to fit them into your daily schedule. Make time in your day for happiness, enjoyment, companionship, rest, thankfulness, and compassion. You'll definitely be happy if you make these things a habit.

Positive emotions behave like nutrition, as we are discovering. While feelings of happiness, appreciation, or peace may appear transitory and insignificant, science is demonstrating that these emotions have an impact on how our brains function, allowing our mindsets to expand and become more adaptable. We develop our resiliency and resourcefulness as we have more of these times of expanded awareness. The "broaden-and-build theory of good emotions," which I developed, explains the hidden worth of positive emotions and how even seemingly insignificant moments of joy add up to make us better people.

What surprises me the most is how regular exposure to happy emotions strengthens and toughens our physical hearts. Cartoon hearts commonly spring to mind when we think about love and positivity. However, it's possible that when we laugh or grin alongside someone else, our cardiovascular systems are each receiving a small tune-up. More generally speaking, micro-moments of shared happiness promote sentiments of safety in our communities in addition to these advantages for physical health. These interactions gradually foster loyalty and trust.

4.

GET IN SHAPE, SHARPEN YOUR IMAGE

Men who are in fantastic form receive more dates than those who are not. It's because excellent bodies—and, let's be honest, good fashion sense—are less common than they once were. Even just being well-groomed will make you stand out and make you more appealing to women.

Exercise and lift. The effort you put out here will more than pay for itself. It goes without saying that guys who take care of their bodies are more appealing to women.

Additionally, in the era of online dating, the profile pictures you choose have a significant impact on how other people see you.

Men who are in fantastic form receive more dates than those who are not. It's because excellent bodies—and, let's be honest, good fashion sense—are less common than they once were. Even just being well-groomed will make you stand out and make you more appealing to women.

Exercise and lift. The effort you put out here will more than pay for itself. It goes without saying that guys who take care of their bodies are more appealing to women.

Additionally, in the era of online dating, the profile pictures you choose have a significant impact on how other people see you.

Your ex suddenly runs into you and turns to face you. You certainly don't want him or her to think of you as being unattractive. Therefore, start considering your appearance more seriously and be ready for it.

Start dressing more formally, take better care of your skin, and get a new haircut to achieve this. A big grin on your face could also be beneficial.

Additionally, looking well contributes to your overall wellbeing. Your objective to make your ex envious will be made possible by an increase in the chance of women connecting with you.

Some people just lack the time and enthusiasm to devote to enhancing their overall appearance, while others occasionally get indifferent about their personal appearance. If you found that you were rusty after your relationship ended, this should inspire you to make some lifestyle adjustments. Understand why? Because our actions outside have an impact on how we feel inside. It's also among the simplest ways to enrage your ex-girlfriend.

Make positive changes in your appearance. Become the person you were when you first met. Do things you enjoyed doing when you were single and that make you feel good or confident.

Purchase a couple new outfits, change your haircut, go to the gym, or paint your nails. Make an effort to differ from how your ex recalls you and appear new.

Being the greatest version of yourself is always beneficial, even while you don't want to change who you are to get your ex back (since ultimately they will leave again, as the real you needs to come back at some time). You might strive to recapture the attraction your ex had toward you.

There is nothing that bring people faster than this, people tend to find you more attractive when you are able to control your body, it shows that you are the master of your decisions, thought, minds, body et.c.

You are able to control how your partner see and respect you when you change your body or physique, he/she sees you as a different person and they will want to feel this new you.

Go to the gym today and start losing those fats, build your edges, curves, mind, body and soul, you also take inventory of your image, mindset, and vision, you will learn to appreciate every effort put in getting to the point you are.

It puts you in control of every situation, no matter what happens your partner see that you are capable in handling it even when he/ she isn't there.

When we say you should sharpen you image is simply the way you are is a wow to everyone who knew you before.

Sharpen your image is not only about your look. It encompasses your presence (how you present yourself), your communication abilities, and your digital footprint.

It's possible that appearance matters a lot more than you think. Some people like to scoff at the role personal appearance plays in the workplace. However, since

93% of our communication is visual your appearance is something you should take very carefully.

I'm not talking about being obsessed with image like a celebrity might be. However, a significant part of how others see you is due to your image. How you show up, physically, conveys signals or makes assumptions about your abilities to lead and execute. Your look will validate what your brand stands for

5.

BE HAPPY AND SEE GOOD IN OTHERS

Try not to focus on the past or possible scenarios. If you're happy, your ex-girlfriend will be jealous since she'll assume you don't need or want to see her anymore.

Getting back on track requires going back to your usual schedule. Now that the period for mourning has gone, you should get back to life.

Additionally, happy people are more attractive by nature. If you have an optimistic attitude on life and attempt to see the bright side of everything, she and her friends will notice.

Convincing your ex that nothing has changed in your life will be your first move. And without them, you could live a happy life. Do whatever you used to do before the split, such as going shopping, hanging out with friends, etc.

It's important because your ex anticipated that you would be depressed; instead of living up to their expectations, you should exude a sense of freedom and vigor. If your ex saw you happy in life, they would be jealous.

If you combine the other recommendations with this one, the result is wonderful.

The emotional turmoil that accompanies a breakup may have a long-term effect on your behavior. You want to avoid caving in. Many people, whether men or women, seek their ex after a split.

They phone them in the middle of the night, send them furious texts, and write them nasty letters. This is horrible conduct.

If your ultimate objective is to let go of bad feelings, this choice can provide some solace. However, it is doubtful that anyone will find someone who is obviously uncomfortable and unable to control their conduct attractive. What then should you do?

Don’t let the trauma of your past relationship, make you believe everyone out there are all the same. It could make you lose the beauty of what you are about to achieve, however learn to tread carefully in letting your heart or emotions out, that is if you are not wanting to let your ex back in your life.

Relationships is all about risk taking, same things in business and its also what makes life beautiful and desirous of the pleasure it gives.

And note sometime the fault could be from you, you have to be ready to work on yourself, to let go of some unwanted issues that your partners also talk about.

Learn to make sacrifices to get your spouse back.

People who learn to appreciate the good in others are more likely to be upbeat and to feel happiness more intensely. We must challenge our presumptions in order to see the good in others, but the effort is worthwhile.

We've had a long time to create ideas about other people. Some of these are reasonable, while others are merely the result of our own prejudices. Therefore, we need to remind ourselves to recognize the good in others if we want to discover real pleasure in the second part of our lives.

Though nobody is perfect. No one is perfect, either. Even your closest pals are not perfect. And even your adversaries are not all bad. On a scale from zero to the ideal human, everyone falls somewhere in between.

This is why you should treat everyone the same way. You should disregard the negative and solely focus on the positive. And there are valid justifications for it.

It goes beyond simply being upbeat and patient with everyone. It is possible to change your life by only seeing the best in others.

Darkness doesn't exist, first of all. Simply said, there is no light. Because of this, you turn on the lights rather than turning off the darkness when you enter a room that is dark.

Everyone is good at birth. Every single individual has the capacity to be excellent from birth. If such potential is not developed, just the absence of good is left. Simply said, "Bad" people haven't yet matured into their positive traits.

Therefore, the only thing you should consider when you see someone is what they have rather than what they lack. Imagining everyone as a starry sky Consider the stars rather than the void. Even if there aren't many stars in them.

You can only succeed if you see the best in other people. You feel content and connected if they share your ideals and character traits. They inspire you and serve as an example if they are better at something than you are.

On the other side, you can only lose if you focus on someone's flaws. You have bad feelings about them. You begin to think you are better than them when you are not. The worst part is that you spend less time correcting your own mistakes.

The truth is that most of us ignore the idea that we still have a long way to go because we feel good about being a few levels ahead of others.

If we look for faults, it is a waste of time to feel good about ourselves. We are made aware of how far we still have to go when we try to see the best in others.

That energy transforms into a genuine pleasant mood when you only see the best in other people. Your interactions with others will be affected. They'll believe that being with you means that they are liked and valued.

This is excellent for both social engagements and daily encounters. The person at the other end of the counter, the delivery guy, and the security officer. Genuine admiration for everyone you encounter arises from being able to see the good in them. You'll instinctively thank folks and grin. They'll think highly of you as well.

This also contributes to your general success in life. When you make others feel appreciated around you, your clients, boss, business partners, and coworkers will value you more. You will inevitably have more possibilities in life as a result of the relationships you build.

In a nut shell what is meant is that no matter what happen between you and your spouse you should always carry the memory you both shared always because that what define who you are and how much love you can give.

6.

VISIT EXCITING PLACES AND POST PHOTOS TO SOCIAL MEDIA

Take images of yourself at new areas you've never been and share them on social media. Your ex-girlfriend can develop resentment over the fact that they broke up and she was unable to accompany you.

This advice will be even more useful if you can also capture pictures of yourself with other people, especially ladies. You may support your ex-girlfriend by demonstrating that you are not alone.

You might also wish to visit some of the sights and tourist attractions in the region where she currently resides or once resided. This is a great approach to have her think about both of you at the same time (to show her you are having fun while helping her associate with you by doing it where she calls home.)

Send Her a Text That Was "By Mistake" Meant for another Girl

An effective approach to make your ex-girlfriend envious is to get a message intended for another female. It's also one of the riskiest actions you can make, though. I advise you to use this as a last option only. All you have to do to make it appear accidental is send her a text message that was meant for another lady (actual or made up).

Sending vulgar or offensive text messages is not advised. Keep it uncomplicated and harmless. E.G., "Bring my hat over later; I left it at your place. Cheers!"

If you start dating the first person you see, you run the danger of your relationship ending before your ex learns about it. If you must have someone with you, make sure you feel at ease in their presence.

If you're fortunate enough to have met someone new who is romantically interested in you, it will make your ex envious and boost your confidence. Additionally, if you're single, give your life more color. Visit with friends, go somewhere, and join a gym. Show your ex how lovely and happy you are to be living without them.

One can benefit greatly by traveling to various locations. Making new acquaintances, having new experiences, and telling fresh tales are all on the list.

You learn more about the local population, including their culture, history, and background, when you start exploring new locations.

Traveling has been shown to boost creativity and general wellness, according to studies. As a result, you should take a break from your regular obligations at work, busy schedule, and daily stress at least once a year. With an open schedule, plan a trip to a new place and let life show you all the options.

Stress and strain are a part of everyone's lives. Visiting places makes us momentarily disengage from our daily routine, which makes us more appreciative of the people and things we already have. We never truly appreciate what we have until we lose it, according to a proverb.

It is said that the mind becomes more creative when a person steps outside of their comfort zone. You need to go to different locations and break out of your everyday routine in order to create new brain connections that result in novel and creative thinking.

You may interact with individuals from other cultures when traveling, which forces you out of your comfort zone. This enables you to approach problems and day-to-day difficulties from a new perspective.

You will develop confidence and peace of mind by being in an unfamiliar environment. You will have the capacity to overcome challenges, which will boost your confidence and also help improve your love life.

Traveling strengthens your relationships and help creates memories that should be posted on you social media platform thereby making your ex wish he/she was close to you to experience such fun and excitement, especially if you go with friends and family. By making photo albums or posting pictures on social media, you may also preserve priceless memories.

There will always be a period when the child inside of you wants to have some fun, regardless of how young or old you are. When you visit locations like hotels in Las Vegas, you don't have to care what you do and may just deviate from the standard.

The health advantages of traveling are enormous, ranging from reducing stress to decreasing your risk of acquiring heart disease. Even if you may spend the entire day in a chair at work, adding some walking to your journey will undoubtedly help your body feel better. Traveling the world can even be a treatment for sadness and anxiety for certain people. Although it's not a certain remedy, it could make you feel better physically and mentally.

7

BE NICE AND SIMPLE

First and foremost, you need to stop talking to your ex through any and all channels. Your ex will eventually attempt to get in touch with you to apologize for breaking up with you. They didn't want to harm you or do anything like.

You should effectively handle such a circumstance rather than responding emotionally. I can claim that my life is better now than it was before and that everything worked out for the best. Keep things basic throughout the chat.

Behave well toward your ex. How are you doing, please? Are you okay? Your Ex will be surprised if you ask them that since they were expecting you to be angry with them.

When you see your ex with a new spouse, avoid being envious.

Keep them from succeeding by letting their jealousy card play. Therefore, you must fully disregard it every time you see your ex with a new girl or boy.

Be yourself when you do reach out to your ex. Be composed and courteous if you do run into one another. This will demonstrate to your ex that you have recovered from your breakup and are at peace.

Avoid dwelling on regrettable or negative previous events when speaking. Instead, recall the happy moments you had together, such as the time you tried an exciting adventure, took a trip, or reserved a luxury restaurant. It can bring back memories for your ex and feel nostalgic.

Avoid being overly anxious to prove that you are still the same person you were before when you run into your ex. They must realize that you are who you are right now. Be authentic, even if it means that since you last saw each other, you have changed.

Show your love, but be discreet about it. Send them a card or a birthday or Christmas wish. Don't overdo it! These little actions will convey to them that they continue to retain a particular place in your heart.

You could occasionally wish to mend fences with your ex or restart your relationship after a separation. You could even be curious about how to make your ex miss you. Remember to give yourself enough time to reflect and adjust to the new circumstances while you work out how to keep your relationship together. Avoid stalking your ex, meet new people, take care of yourself, and participate in your interests if you still think getting back in touch with your ex-boyfriend or ex-girlfriend is a smart option. Both your ex and a newer version of yourself will be drawn to it. Keep in mind to have fun during the process and gently prod your ex to feel the same way.

You need to keep your emotions in check and get ready for situations like these.

Say you want your ex-girlfriend to regret leaving you. Display your poise and composure for her. Act as though you're at that place even if you're not. Make sure you don't take this game too far. When you see your ex-girlfriend on the street, try not to be overly happy or irritated.

She/he can't be duped into thinking you don't harbor any hatred. Use the phrases "disappointed" or "sad that it didn't work out" if she/he brings up the subject of the breakup. They make it sound as though you expected your relationship to endure, but in reality, you're able to accept your ex's decision to end things, and you want to go on with your life.

8.

BECOME SUCCESSFUL

Not to worry. You don't need to be awarded the Nobel Prize to make your ex-regret breaking up with you. But it is unquestionably an unexpected turn of events to become more successful than you were. Perhaps your ex failed to see a quality in you, like a rare ability. Both the mystery and a new career or interest are alluring.

How can you make yourself seem more successful? Consider your talents first. For instance, you could desire to launch a small business that you have put off for a long time for a number of different reasons.

Are you an authority in certain fields? If yes, consider starting a blog and providing your visitors with useful content. Even changing careers might make your ex-girlfriend regret leaving you or make your ex-boyfriend become curious about your personal life.

How will your ex learn about your accomplishments? The greatest possibilities are usually mutual friends and social media profiles. It's conceivable that your pals may mistakenly or purposely share exciting news with your ex. It will work in any case.

This topic is one that many people will not agree to, but it's important and its always a hidden silent topic. But your status changing from what was known about you is really sexy and desirous, it makes your partner feels they are really missing out on the experience of living a large than life status.

Your change in status will bring you before new people of class and introduce you to different level of greatness, where your partner wish to experience the life you are living, because you too had your lives plan and you had wishes and desires and now it's unraveling before your partner eye and they can't experience it with you.

And its hurtful to see that they can't share in that with you, that's the pain they will have to bear, which will draw them back to you and make them want you back.

9.

ENJOY YOUR FREE LIFE

You undoubtedly ask yourself, "How can I enjoy life if I am continuously thinking about my ex, can't sleep, and can't concentrate?" So let me ask you this in response: "Do you appreciate living in this emotional quagmire, gradually losing your zest for life?"

She wouldn't want to see a worse-off version of you again, girlfriend. It isn't sexual. Only if you start enjoying your life will you be able to make her regret harming you.

Likewise, your quick recuperation will perplex and excite your ex-boyfriend. So maybe it's time to adjust your perspective and resume living a full life?

You will continue to be emotionally reliant on your ex as long as you cling to the past. You set up a scenario in which other individuals have power over your emotions. However, you must turn it the opposite way. So start appreciating who you are and what you do. Keep it real; else, your ex will see right through you. Instead, engage in enjoyable activities like hiking, drawing, and guitar playing.

Be nice to yourself and develop the ability to recognize the inner beauty that your ex failed to perceive. Your excellent traits will eventually be apparent to everyone in your vicinity. And if your ex-boyfriend or ex-girlfriend decides not to take you back after that, they are not deserving of having you and will never provide you happiness. Therefore, why would you waste time with them?

If you deal with neediness, your sense of self-worth may be a little low. You may be hoping your ex would help you feel better about yourself, but the truth is that only you have the power to accomplish that. You shouldn't rely on other people to make you happy. It causes them to feel guilty, responsible, and ultimately, resentful of you.

Self-worth is the idea that you are a valuable person and that you are good enough just the way you are. Instead of searching for someone else to complete you or make your life worthwhile when it comes to relationships, it's crucial to feel entire and complete on your own.

You can have a rather poor sense of self-worth if you cope with neediness. Although you might have hoped your ex would make you feel better about yourself, the fact is that only you have the ability to do so. To be happy, you shouldn't need other people's approval. They become guilty, responsible, and eventually resentful of you as a result.

Self-worth is the conviction that you are a worthwhile individual and are sufficient in your current state. It's important to feel whole and complete on your own, rather than looking on others to make you feel full or give your life meaning in terms of relationships.

You don't need to prove anything to anyone, and your life is not a contest. The aforementioned advice will ultimately help you reach your objective if your main goal is to get your ex back. To be confident that your partner truly cares about you and isn't just using you as a handy backup while searching for a better choice, check with your boyfriend or girlfriend.

10.

LEARN TO SAY SORRY.

Think deeply about anything you did or didn't do that somehow contributed to the downfall of the relationship, and clean the slate by giving your ex a proper apology. Take full responsibility for the offense, without blaming your ex, giving excuses, or expecting an apology (or even forgiveness) in return. It may very well be that your ex contributed to the situation, but you cannot apologize for someone else; you can only apologize for yourself. Leave him or her out of it and odds are the apology will be reciprocated.

Avoid using the word "but." "I am sorry, but..." means "I am not sorry." Also, do not say "I'm sorry you feel that way" or "I'm sorry if you were offended." This makes it seem like you are blaming the other person, and is not a real apology.

A true apology should be structured as follows: **Regret, Responsibility**, and Remedy. The first step indicates that you are sorry for what you've done. The second step puts the responsibility on you without making excuses or blaming someone else. The final step offers to make it right or change your behavior in the future. For example: "I just wanted to apologize for when I blew you off all those times that you wanted to spend with me. You must've really felt neglected. I'm going to try really hard from now on, to make it a point to do more things with you so you won't feel like that again. I'm glad you gave me your point of view to realize that."

The reason there are too many divorce all over the world today is because so many people don't know how to apologize to their spouse's, everyone believe they are perfect in their own eyes not looking at the pain or emotional torture they are inflicting on their partners, sometimes unknowingly, but to be truly sorry or apologetic we must learn to understand our partner emotional state, thereby bringing about true relationship or love.

Everyone has the responsibility to understand the changes in your relationship or in the lives of your spouse because that will only prove that you are in whatever pain or challenges they are facing and you are ready to go through it with them. Never underestimate the little thing or actions from your spouse before it build up to become something you can't control.

So to enjoy your relationship or love life you must be in every situation your partner is, i.e. stand by them, never belittle them in their time of challenge or difficulties.

And we must always learn to speak up in every giving opportunity and make sure that they understand.

Relationship isn't built by only one person but by two determined spouse ready to face the world together.

Conclusion

Do you recall the time you spent reflecting following your breakup? Well, that should be useful right now. Remind yourself of what went wrong when you're back with your lover and work to avoid it in the future. If your excessive fighting was the issue, then try to calm down whenever the temptation to fight arises. Try to be friendlier this time if your issue was that you were rude to his buddies; your boyfriend should be worth it.

Remind your ex that whatever he is doing is causing the same issue as last time if he is the one making the blunders.

Even while you should try to avoid repeating them, if you are continuously fixated on doing so, you won't be able to enjoy the relationship. Unless there is a disagreement, just have fun and try not to worry about it too much. You won't be able to live in the moment if you're constantly concerned that you'll lose him again.

Your ex will be able to detect if you're worried about the relationship ending once more, which will make him worry even more.

If you can’t get your loved one back, stop wasting time and start living for yourself.

Once you begin enjoying who you are, you will no longer want to bring back relationships with someone who didn’t appreciate you in the first place.

Not every relationship must end successful, once you understand this you stop forcing thing, sometimes someone leaving you is for the better.

If your partner is proving not to look or come back after applying these method, you should let them go and move on with your life, someone better will find you.

www.ingramcontent.com/pod-product-compliance
Lightning Source LLC
LaVergne TN
LVHW080558160826
845677LV00010B/1902

* 9 7 9 8 3 5 1 6 1 1 9 0 7 *